The Perfect
Wedding
Songbook

Compiled by Len Handler
Associate Music Editor: Edwin McLean
Music Engraving by Edwin McLean and W.R. Music
Copy Editor: Cathy Cassinos-Carr
Production Manager: Daniel Rosenbaum
Art Direction: Kerstin Fairbend
Administration: Monica Corton
Director of Music: Mark Phillips

ISBN: 0-89524-633-3

CONTENTS

PRELUDE MUSIC

Air (from *Water Music Suite*) — Handel — 10

Canon In D — Pachelbel — 12

Jesu, Joy Of Man's Desiring — Bach — 15

Elegie — Massenet — 18

Amazing Grace — Traditional — 20

Sleepers, Wake — Bach — 22

Minuets I & II — Purcell — 26

Theme From Romeo And Juliet — Tschaikovsky — 28

Air — Mozart — 31

Minuet (from *Anna Magdalena Notebook*) — Bach — 32

Air On A G String — Bach — 34

Chorale (from *Anna Magdalena Notebook*) — Bach — 36

PROCESSIONAL MUSIC

Bridal Chorus (from *Lohengrin*) — Wagner — 38

Wedding March (from *A Midsummer Night's Dream*) — Mendelssohn — 40

Trumpet Tune — Clarke — 42

Allegro Maestoso — Handel — 43

March — Handel — 44

Prince Of Denmark's March — Clarke — 46

Processional (from *Royal Fireworks Music*) — Handel — 47

Processional (from *St. Anthony Chorale*) — Haydn — 48

Rondeau/The Masterpiece (arr. Parnes) — Mouret — 50

Processional (from *Water Music Suite*) — Handel — 54

INTERLUDE MUSIC: TRADITIONAL

Sarabande In E Minor — Handel — 56

Sarabande (from *Anna Magdalena Notebook*) — Bach — 58

Ave Maria (adapted by Gounod) — Bach — 60

Ave Maria — Schubert — 64

Aria (Willst Du Dein Herz Mir Schenken) — Bach — 70

Adagio (trans. by Bach) — Marcello — 72

The Lord's Prayer	Talbot	75
O Lord Most Holy (Panis Angelicus)	Franck	76
Sarabande In D Minor	Handel	80
Be Thou With Me (Bist Du Bei Mir)	Bach	81
My Faithful Heart (Mein Glaubiges Herz)	Bach	84

INTERLUDE MUSIC: CONTEMPORARY

The Battle Hymn Of Love	Overstreet, Schlitz	89
A Love Until The End Of Time	Connors, Holdridge	93
May You Always	Markes, Charles	96
Melody Of Love	Glazer, Engelmann	100
Forever And Ever, Amen	Overstreet, Schlitz	102
For Sure, For Certain, Forever, For Always	Webb	106
Annie's Song	Denver	108
Lady	Richie	112
My Treasure	Brown	116
Goin' Gone	Koller, Alger, Dale	120
I Do	Alger, Longacre	124
Everything True Love Touches	Alger, Sanders	128
From This Moment On	Wildhorn, Goodrum	132
I Do	Wildhorn	136
Hold On To The Nights	Marx	140
We've Only Just Begun	Williams, Nichols	146
Nobody Loves Me Like You Do	Phillips, Dunne	149
You Are So Beautiful	Preston, Fisher	154
The Love Of Loving You	Paxton	157
Truly	Richie	160
All My Life	Bonoff	163
This Very Day	Overstreet, Elliott	166
Love Chooses You	Lewis	169
Love Can Build A Bridge	Overstreet, Judd, Jarvis	174
Call The Preacher	Overstreet	179
I Fell In Love With You For Life	Morgan, Davis	182
The Keeper Of Your Heart	Morgan, Davis	185
For You	Denver	189
Perhaps Love	Denver	193
Angel Eyes	Hiatt, Koller	196

RECESSIONAL MUSIC

Hallelujah Chorus (from *Messiah*) Handel 200

Allegro Boyce 202

Voluntary On The Doxology (Old 100th) Purcell 206

Hornpipe Handel 211

Fanfares Mouret 214

POSTLUDE MUSIC

Adagio (from *Water Music Suite*) Handel 218

Andante (from *Water Music Suite*) Handel 220

Larghetto Handel 222

Prelude In C (from *The Well-Tempered Clavier, Part I*) Bach 224

Wedding Music:
A Complete Guide

Music: A Key Player
On Your Wedding Day

Music is one of the most important aspects of your wedding. Not only does it add a deeply personal touch, it is a key factor in creating the ambience you want.

That's why it's important to take special care in choosing the songs for your wedding—and in choosing who will play them.

This book is designed to help you do both.

The Ceremony

The following is a general outline of a traditional wedding ceremony. Music for each portion of the ceremony can be found grouped according to category starting on page 10.

1. <u>Prelude music</u> (while guests are being seated; approximately 20 minutes)
2. <u>Processional</u> (while the wedding party enters)
3. <u>Interlude music</u> (select interlude music for the following portions of the ceremony):
   - **a)** Father gives the bride away
   - **b)** Bride and groom's charges
   - **c)** vows
   - **d)** ring ceremony
   - **e)** meditational or prayer
   - **f)** pronouncement of marriage
   - **g)** announcement
4. <u>Recessional</u> (the wedding party files out)
5. <u>Postlude</u> (the guests follow)

Before selecting songs, be sure to consult your clergy regarding any possible musical restrictions.

Hiring Musicians:
The Ceremony

If music for the ceremony conjures up visions of Mrs. Peabody playing "I Love You Truly" on the organ, think again. These days, just about anything goes.

That's not meant to knock the old-fashioned approach. Perhaps an organist or keyboardist will suit your needs perfectly. But consider your options. Many wedding songs—even the most traditional—sound beautiful on instruments such as classical guitar, violin, harp, recorder, flute, or a combination. Flute and classical guitar, for instance, sound especially intimate and lovely together, and it's a popular combination for wedding ceremonies. (Note: All music in this book is arranged for keyboard, but may also be adapted for any of the aforementioned instrumental combinations.)

To find musicians for the ceremony, try your local music store, musicians' union, music departments of colleges and universities, or symphony offices. Of course, the yellow pages are also an obvious source, but can be risky. Word-of-mouth referrals are always best; in their absence, try to obtain references.

A word of caution: Make every effort to see the musicians perform *before* you sign on the dotted line. A tape of their music is not always a valid representation.

Hiring Musicians:
The Reception

In general, the guidelines for hiring musicians for the ceremony also apply to hiring a band for the reception. But here are a few additional tips.

Many large catering houses present monthly showcases in which as many as a dozen bands, orchestras, and entertainers each present a 15-20 minute performance. This is an especially good way to hear a variety of styles (and bands).

Please note, however, that many different bands can operate under the same name. So be sure you know which version of the band you're hiring!

On this matter and others, a contract (usually supplied by the band or booking agent) will help to protect you. Make sure it addresses the following questions:

1. How many musicians are in the band?
2. If you first saw the band at a wedding showcase, will it be the same lineup (including the lead vocalist)?
3. Can they play the special songs you require, as well as requests at the reception?
4. Will the bandleader also act as Master of Ceremonies?
5. How will the musicians be dressed?
6. What will be the complete cost for the band? Overtime rate? When and how do they expect to be paid? Is there a deposit required?
7. Backup in case of emergency?

Wedding Checklist

Six months before

___ 1. Select clergy
___ 2. Select and reserve ceremony site
___ 3. Select and book reception site (in some areas of the country, allow 12-18 months)
___ 4. Select and book caterer (in some areas of the country, allow 12-18 months)
___ 5. Secure accommodations for out-of-town members of the wedding party
___ 6. Book honeymoon accommodations
___ 7. Select and book florist
___ 8. Order bride's dress
___ 9. Order bridesmaids dresses
___ 10. Compile invitation list
___ 11. Book musician(s) for ceremony
___ 12. Book soloist or singer(s) for ceremony
___ 13. Book musicians (band) for reception (in some areas of the country, allow 12-18 months)

Three months before

___ 1. Register for gifts
___ 2. Select photograph for wedding announcement
___ 3. Select and order invitations
___ 4. Select photographer
___ 5. Select music for ceremony
___ 6. Plan rehearsal dinner
___ 7. Buy wedding rings
___ 8. Book limousine or car service

Two months before

___ 1. Address and mail invitations (generally, about six weeks prior to wedding)
___ 2. Select gifts for wedding party
___ 3. Buy marriage license
___ 4. Buy bridal accessories
___ 5. Coordinate attire for best man and ushers

One month before

___ 1. Send wedding photo and announcement to newspaper
___ 2. Meet with caterer
___ 3. Meet with florist
___ 4. Meet with musicians regarding ceremony music
___ 5. Meet with bandleader regarding reception music
___ 6. Confirm honeymoon arrangements
___ 7. Confirm accommodations for out-of-town guests
___ 8. Meet with clergy about service

One week-10 days before

Call to reconfirm with:
___ caterer
___ florist
___ musicians
___ photographer
___ limo/car service

Prelude Music

Air

from *Water Music Suite*

George Frideric Handel

Canon In D

Johann Pachelbel

Jesu, Joy Of Man's Desiring

Johann Sebastian Bach

Andante cantabile

Elegie

Jules Massenet

dim. e rit.

Amazing Grace*

Traditional

*May be used as prelude or interlude music.

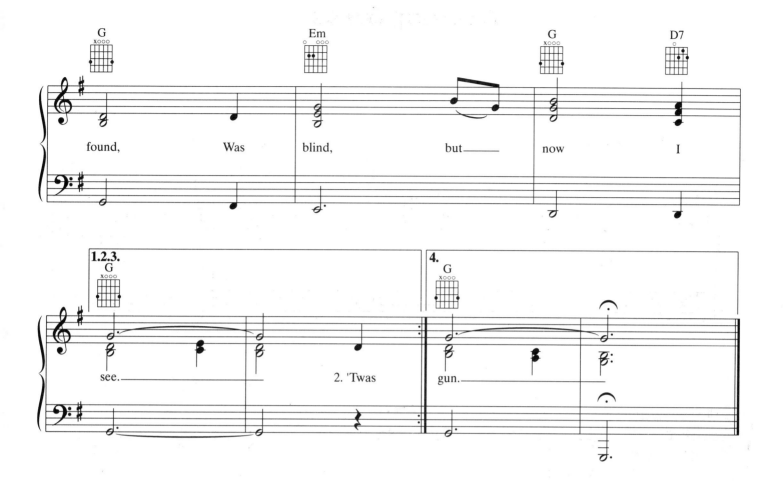

Additional Lyrics

2. 'Twas grace that taught my heart to fear,
   And grace my fears relieved;
   How precious did that grace appear
   The hour I first believed!

3. Through many dangers, toils, and snares,
   I have already come;
   'Tis grace hath brought me safe thus far,
   And grace will lead me home.

4. When we've been there ten thousand years,
   Bright shining as the sun,
   We've no less days to sing God's praise
   Than when we first begun.

Sleepers, Wake*

Johann Sebastian Bach

*May be used as prelude or interlude music.

Minuets I & II

Henry Purcell

MINUET I

Allegretto

MINUET II

Theme From Romeo And Juliet

Peter Il'yich Tschaikovsky

Andante cantabile

cresc. poco a poco

Air

Wolfgang Amadeus Mozart

Minuet

from *Anna Magdalena Notebook*

Johann Sebastian Bach

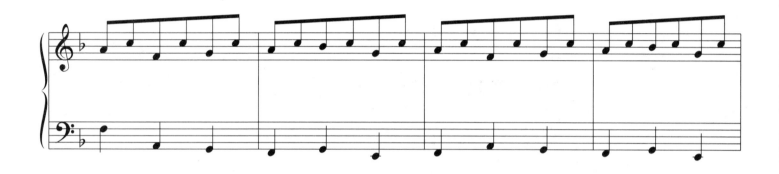

Air On A G String

Johann Sebastian Bach

Chorale

from *Anna Magdalena Notebook*

Johann Sebastian Bach

Processional Music

Bridal Chorus

from *Lohengrin*

Richard Wagner

Wedding March

from *A Midsummer Night's Dream*

Felix Mendelssohn

Allegro marcia

Trumpet Tune

Jeremiah Clarke

Allegro Maestoso

George Frideric Handel

March

George Frideric Handel

Prince Of Denmark's March

Jeremiah Clarke

Processional

from *Royal Fireworks Music*

George Frideric Handel

Processional

from *St. Anthony Chorale*

Franz Joseph Haydn

Rondeau
The Masterpiece
as featured on the television series Masterpiece Theatre

Jean-Joseph Mouret
arr. by Paul Parnes

Majestically (Not Fast)

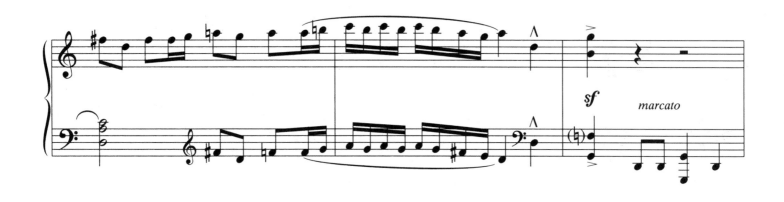

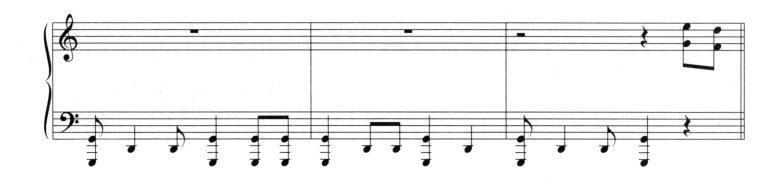

Processional

from *Water Music Suite*

George Frideric Handel

Andante

Interlude Music

Sarabande In E Minor

George Frideric Handel

Sarabande

from *Anna Magdalena Notebook*

Johann Sebastian Bach

Ave Maria

Johann Sebastian Bach
adapted by Charles Gounod

Andante con moto

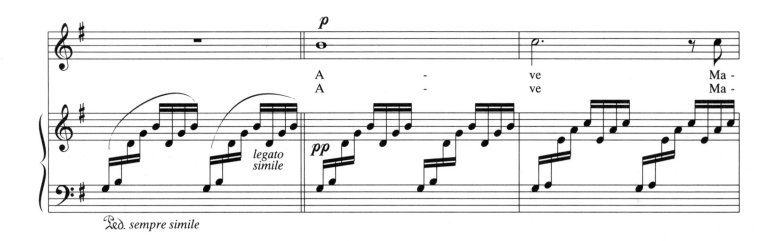

Ave Maria

Franz Joseph Schubert

Molto lento

A — ve Ma - ri — a! gra - ti - a —— ple -

na, Ma - ri — a,— gra - ti - a ple - na, Ma - ri — a, gra - ti - a ple-

na, A - ve,_____ A - ve! Do - mi - nus,_____ Do - mi - nus— te - cum. Be - ne -

di - cta tu in mu - li - e - ri - bus, et be - ne - di - ctus, et

be - ne - di - ctus fru - ctus ven - tris, ven - tris tu - i, Je - sus.

fp *pp*

A - ve Ma - ri - a!

ho - ra mor - tis no - strae, in ho - ra mor - tis, mor - tis no - strae, in

ho - ra mor - tis no - strae. A - ve Ma - ri -

a! A - ve Ma - ri - a! gra - ti - a ple -

na, Ma - ri - a,— gra - ti - a ple - na, Ma - ri - a, gra - ti - a - ple-

na, A - ve, - A - ve! Do - mi - nus,——— Do - mi - nus— te cum; Be - ne-

di - cta tu in mu - li - e - ri bus, et be - ne - di - ctus, et

be - ne - di - ctus fru - ctus ven - tris, ventris tu - i, Je - sus.

A - ve Ma - ri - a!

Aria
(Willst Du Dein Herz Mir Schenken)

Johann Sebastian Bach

schließ die größ - ten Freu - den in dei - nem Her - zen ein.

Additional Lyrics

2. Behutsam sei and schweige, und traue keiner Wand,
Ließ' innerlich und zeige dich außen unbekannt.
Kein Argwohn mußt du geben, Verstellung nötig ist,
Genug, daß du, mein Leben, der Treu' versichert bist.

3. Begehre keine Blicke von meiner Liebe nicht,
Der Neid hat viele Stücke auf unser Tun gericht't.
Du mußt die Brust verschließen, hal't' deine Neigung ein,
Die Lust, die wir genießen, muß ein Geheimnis sein.

4. Zu frei sein, sich ergehen, hat oft Gefahr gebracht,
Man muß sich wohl verstehen, weil ein falsch Auge wacht.
Du mußt den Spruch bedenken, den ich zuvor getan;
Willst du dein Herz mir schenken, so fang es heimlich an.

Adagio

Alessandro Marcello
trans. by Johann Sebastian Bach

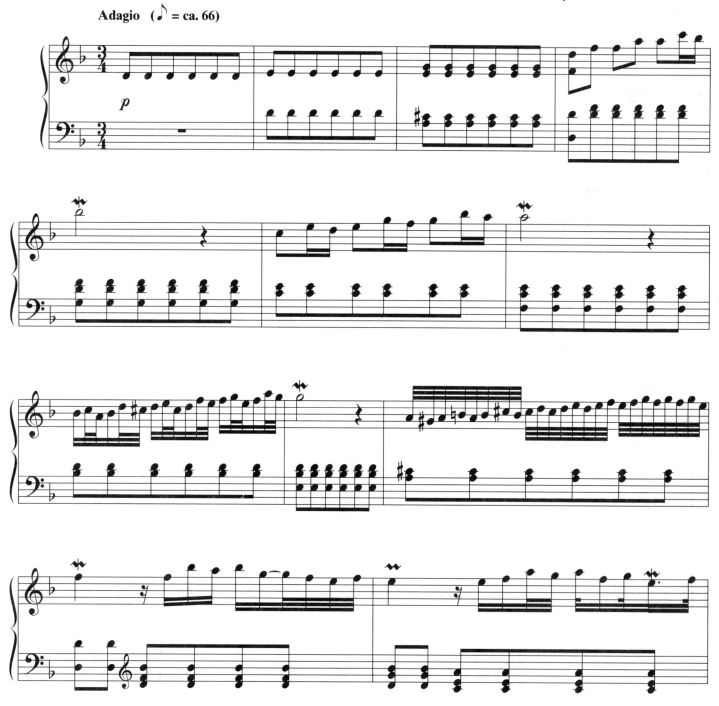

The Lord's Prayer

Music by John Michael Talbot
Lyrics adapted from The Liturgy

O Lord Most Holy
(Panis Angelicus)

Cesar Franck

O lov - ing Fa - ther, Thee would we be prais - ing
Dat pa - nis coe - li - cus fi - gu - ris ter - mi -

al - ways. Help us to know Thee, know Thee and
num. O res mi - ra - bi - lis man - du - cat

love Thee; Fa - ther, Fa - ther, grant us Thy truth and
Do - mi - num, pau - per, pau - per, ser - vus et hu - mi -

grace; Fa - ther, Fa - ther, guide and de - fend
lis, Pau - per, pau - per, (f)ser - vus et hu - mi -

us.
lis.

Rule Thou our wil - ful hearts,
Pa - nis an - ge - li - cus

Keep Thee our
fit pa - nis

wan- d'ring thoughts;
ho - mi - num

In all our sor - rows let us
(f)Dat pa - nis coe - li - cus fi - gu -

find our rest in
ris ter - mi -

Thee;
num,

And in temp - ta - tion's hour,
O res mi - ra - bi - lis

Save through Thy
man - du - cat

Sarabande In D Minor

George Frideric Handel

Be Thou With Me
(Bist Du Bei Mir)

Johann Sebastian Bach

Andante sostenuto e cantabile

soul shall rest in deep re - pose.   My heart is glad
Ster - ben und zu mei - ner Ruh'   Ach, wie is ver - gnügt

When thou art near___ me,   My eye - lids___ closed by thy___ ten - der
wär' so mein En___ de,   Es drück___ ten___ dei - ne schö___ nen___

hands,___ My___ eyes with love will rest on thee.   My heart is
Hän - de mir___ die ge - treu - en Au - gen .zu.   Ach, wie ver -

glad   When thou art near me,   My eye - lids___
gnügt   wär' so mein En - de,   Es drück___ ten___

closed by thy tender hands, My eyes with love will rest on
dei ne schö nen Hän de mir die ge treu en Au gen

thee. Be thou with me,
zu. Bist du bei mir,

My joy and glad - ness, In deep re -
geh' ich mit Freu - den, zum Ster - ben

pose my soul shall rest, My soul shall rest in deep re - pose.
und zu mei ner Ruh, zum Ster - ben und zu mei ner Ruh'.

My Faithful Heart

(Mein Glaubiges Herz)

Johann Sebastian Bach

Andante con moto

Mein gläu - bi-ges Her - ze, froh - lo - cke, sing', scher - ze,
My heart—— ev - er faith - ful, Sing prais - es, be joy - ful,

mein gläu - bi-ges Her - ze, froh-
My heart—— ev - er faith - ful, Sing

lo - cke, sing', scher - ze, froh - lo - cke, sing', scher - ze, dein Je - sus ist nah; mein
prais - es, be joy - ful, sing prais - es, be joy - ful, Thy Je - sus is near; My

gläu - bi - ges Her - ze, froh - lo - cke, sing', sher - ze, fro - lo - cke, sing', scher - ze, dein
heart___ ev - er faith - ful, Sing prais - es, be joy - ful, sing prais - es, be joy - ful, Thy

Je - sus ist nah!
Je - sus is near!

Weg Jam - mer, weg Kla - gen, weg
A - way___ with com - plain - ing, a -

Jam - mer, weg Kla - gen, ich will— euch nur sa - gen, mein Je - sus ist da; weg
way— with com - plain - ing, Faith ev - er main-tain - ing, My Je - sus is here; A -

Jam - mer, weg Kla - gen, ich will— euch nur sa - gen, mein Je - sus ist da, mein—
way— with com - plain - ing, Faith ev - er main-tain - ing, My Je - sus is here, my—

Je - sus ist da;
Je - sus is here;

weg Jam - mer, weg Kla - gen, weg
A - way— with com-plain - ing, a -

scher-ze, froh-lo - cke, sing', scher - ze, mein
joy-ful, sing prais - es, be joy - ful, My

gläu - bi-ges Her - ze, froh-lo - cke, sing', scher - ze froh-lo - cke, sing', scher - ze, dein
heart — ev - er faith-ful, Sing prais - es, be joy - ful, sing prais - es, be joy - ful, Thy

Je - sus ist da!
Je - sus is here!

The Battle Hymn Of Love

Words and Music by
Paul Overstreet and Don Schlitz

will   not   run.____ Till   my   death   I__ will   stand   by__

you.____

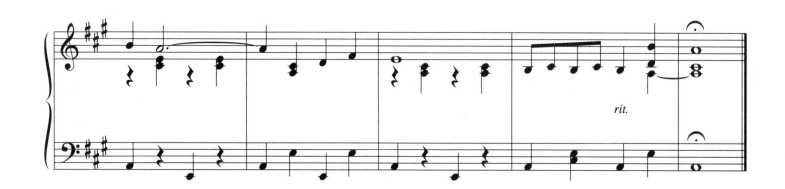

rit.

Additional Lyrics

2. There are wars and there are rumors,
The wars yet to come.
Temptations we'll have to walk through.
Though others may tremble
I will not run.
Till my death I will stand by you.

2nd Chorus:
I will put on the armor of faithfulness
To fight for a heart that is true.
Till the battle is won
I will not rest.
Till my death I will stand by you.

A Love Until The End Of Time

Music by Lee Holdridge
Words by Carol Connors

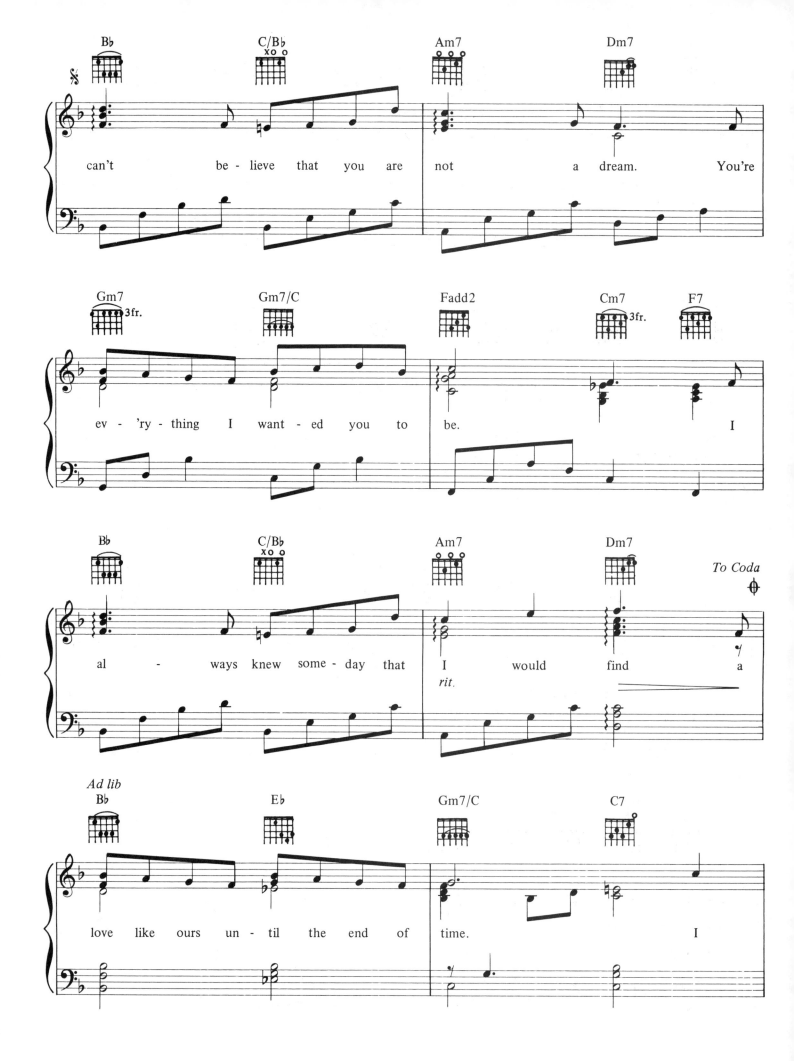

May You Always

Words and Music by
Larry Markes and Dick Charles

Melody Of Love

Words by Tom Glazer
Music by Hans Englemann

Forever And Ever, Amen

Words and Music by
Paul Overstreet and Don Schlitz

er, for - ev - er and ev - er,___ for - ev - er and ev -

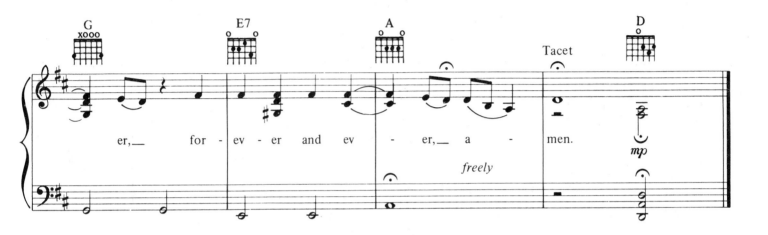

er,___ for - ev - er and ev - er,___ a - men.

freely

Tacet

Additional Lyrics

2. You're not just time that I'm killing.
   I'm no longer one of those guys.
   As sure as I live, this love that I give
   Is gonna be yours until the day that I die. *(To Chorus)*

3. They say time takes its toll on a body,
   Makes a young girl's brown hair turn gray.
   Well honey, I don't care. I ain't in love with your hair.
   And if it all fell out I'd love you anyway.

4. Well, they say time can play tricks on a memory,
   Make people forget things they knew.
   Well, it's easy to see it's happening to me.
   I've already forgotten every woman but you. *(To Chorus)*

For Sure, For Certain, Forever, For Always

Words and Music by
Jimmy Webb

Additional Lyrics

2. And in the darkest night, close together,
   When winter weather cuts like a knife,
   I will still... *(To Chorus)*

3. If the sky should fall and shatter 'round me,
   And fire surround me, through terrors rife,
   I will still... *(To Chorus)*

Annie's Song

Words and Music by
John Denver

Lady

Words and Music by
Lionel Richie

My Treasure

Words and Music by
Scott Wesley Brown

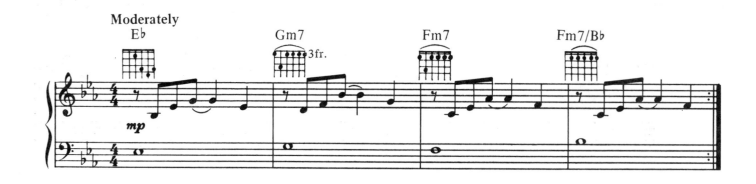

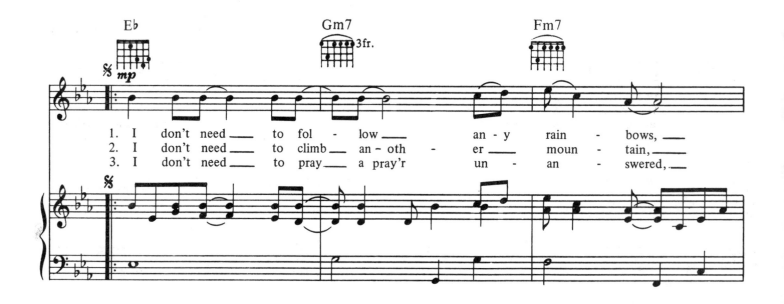

1. I don't need ___ to fol - low ___ an - y rain - bows, ___
2. I don't need ___ to climb ___ an - oth - er ___ moun - tain, ___
3. I don't need ___ to pray ___ a pray'r un - an - swered, ___

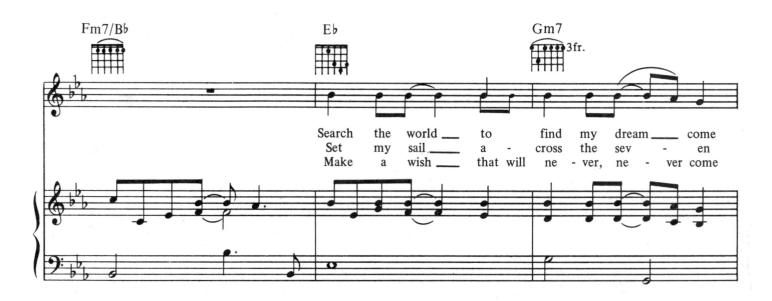

Search the world ___ to find my dream ___ come
Set my sail ___ a - cross the sev - en
Make a wish ___ that will ne - ver, ne - ver come

You.

Trea - sure in You.

Goin' Gone

Words and Music by
Fred Koller, Pat Alger
and Bill Dale

Moderately slow

The light-house stands a - bove the har - bor giv - ing guid - ance with it's light. But I had no one to re - turn

122

I Do

Words and Music by
Pat Alger and Susan Longacre

mo - ment of truth,____ we're for - ev - er bound.____ I knew____ our

first time a - round____ I'd come to love you like I____ do now;____

To Coda
I'll al - ways love you like I____ do now.____

Who sur -

Everything True Love Touches

Words and Music by
Pat Alger and Mark D. Sanders

Additional Lyrics

2. I know this is a precious gift,
   With every touch and tender kiss;
   I watch all the riches of our love unfold.
   And with each day I spend with you,
   Daddy's words still ring true:
   "Everything true love touches turns to gold." *(To Chorus)*

From This Moment On

Words and Music by
Frank Wildhorn and Randy Goodrum

Moderately slow

* Recorded a half step lower

I Do

Words and Music by
Frank Wildhorn

So then here's to us. I give my all to you.

Yes ba-by, I do. _(melody)_ *mp*

Yes ba-by, I do. *rit.*

Additional Lyrics

2. If I could take a star from the sky,
   I'd make it shine on you for the rest of your life.
   Tonight our hearts became one, united forever
   For all of the world to see.
   So baby, it's you and me eternally,
   Everything that we're meant to be. *(To Chorus)*

Hold On To The Nights

Words and Music by
Richard Marx

*Vocalists: Hold C for 4 beats.

142

some-one I've— been search-ing for— is right there.——

Hold on—— to the nights.——

Hold on—— to the mem - o - ries.——

144

I wish that I could give you more.

Oh.

Hold on to the nights.

We've Only Just Begun

Words by Paul Williams
Music by Roger Nichols

Lyric by
PAUL WILLIAMS

1. We've On-ly Just Be - gun to
2. Be - fore the ris - ing sun we
3. 4. And when the eve - ning comes we

live,_____ White lace and prom - i - ses,
fly,_____ So man - y roads to choose,
smile,_____ So much of life a - head,

Nobody Loves Me Like You Do

Words by Pamela Phillips
Music by James P. Dunne

touched my heart_ in plac-es *Girl:* that I nev-er e - ven knew.____

1. No - bod - y loves_ me like you do.

2. *Both:* No - bod - y loves_ me,

no - bod - y loves_ me,

no - bod - y loves_ me like you

℅ 3rd Verse:

Boy: I was words without a tune,
Girl: I was a song still unsung.
Boy: A poem with no rhyme;
Girl: A dancer out of time;
Both: But now there's you.
Nobody loves me like you do.

To Chorus

You Are So Beautiful

Words and Music by
Billy Preston and Bruce Fisher

The Love Of Loving You

Words and Music by
Tom Paxton

158

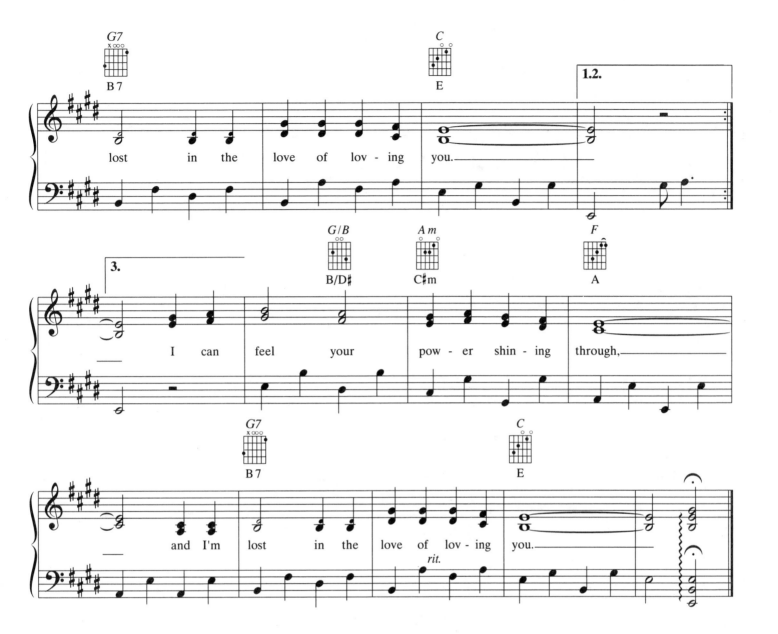

lost in the love of lov-ing you.

1.2.

3.

I can feel your pow-er shin-ing through,

and I'm lost in the love of lov-ing you.

rit.

Additional Lyrics

2. It's so strange, the way we live our lives in sorrow,
   And the ways we let the happiness slip by.
   For our eyes are always fixed upon tomorrow,
   While today is in the corner of our eye. *(To Chorus)*

3. I was looking for tomorrow when you found me,
   And my heart was anywhere but in today.
   Now the magic of the moment's all around me,
   And I hear the words I've always longed to say: *(To Chorus)*

Truly

Words and Music by
Lionel Richie

All My Life

Words and Music by
Karla Bonoff

Moderately

Am I real-ly here in your arms?
And I nev-er real-ly knew how to love,

This is just like I dreamed it would be.
I just hoped some-how I'd see.
Oh, I

I feel like we're fro-zen in time,
asked for a lit-tle help from a-bove,

and you're the on - ly one I can see.

send an an - gel down to me.

Hey, I've looked all my life for you, now you're here.

And hey, I'll spend all my life with you,

all my life.

This Very Day

Words and Music by
Paul Overstreet and John Elliott

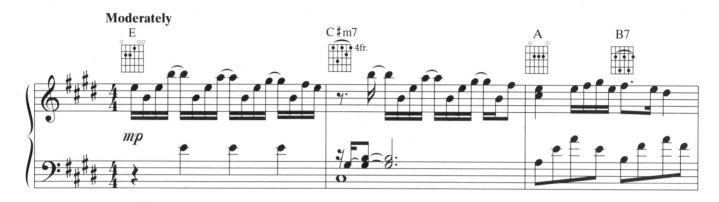

I've been search-ing all— my life— for the
Like the an - swer to— my prayers,— from

wom-an I— was meant— to make— my— wife. And I have kept my
this day on— I'll wake— to find— her— there. And yes, I do be-lieve— in

166

and I will face each ris - ing sun____ nev - er

end-ing what's____ be-gun____ this ver-y day.____

Love Chooses You

Words and Music by
Laurie Lewis

down to your shoes. It knows heart-ache and

trial but ac-cepts no de-ni-al.

You can't choose who you love,— love choos-es you.—

2. In the

Tell— me now if I'm— wrong.—

Chorus

Are__ you feel-in' the same?__

Are__ your feet__ on the ground?__

Are__ you call-ing__ my__ name?__

Do__ you lie a-wake__ nights?__

Please__ say__ you do.__

'Cause_ you can't choose_ who you_ love, love choos- es you._

straight ♪'s

D.S. (with repeat)
al Coda

3. Love

172

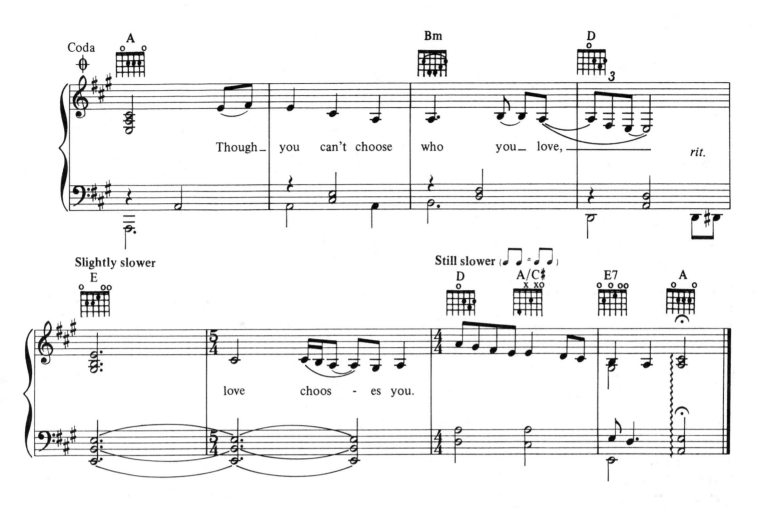

Coda

Though you can't choose who you love, *rit.*

Slightly slower

love choos - es you.

Still slower

Additional Lyrics

2. In the wink of an eye love looses an arrow.
   We control it no more than the flight of the sparrow,
   The swell of the tide or the light of the moon.
   You can't choose who you love, love chooses you. *(To Chorus)*

3. Love cuts like a torch to a heart behind steel,
   And though you may hide it, love knows how you feel.
   And though you may trespass on the laws of the land,
   Your heart has to follow when love takes your hand.

4. And it seems we're two people within the same circle;
   It's drawn tighter and tighter till you're all that I see.
   I'm full and I'm empty and you're pouring through me
   Like a warm rain fallin' through the leaves on a tree. *(To Chorus)*

Love Can Build A Bridge

Words and Music by
Paul Overstreet, Naomi Judd
and John Jarvis

1. I'd glad-ly walk a-cross— the des - ert with no— shoes up-on— my feet— to
2. See additional lyrics

share with you——— the last— bite——— of bread— I had— to eat.— I would

swim out— to save you in your sea of bro - ken dreams.——— When

* Recorded a half step lower.

all your hopes— are sink-ing, let me show you what love—means. Love can build a
er.

bridge be-tween your heart and mine.

Love can build a bridge, don't you think— it's time?— Don't you think— it's time?—

Additional Lyrics

2. I would whisper love so loudly,
   Every heart would understand
   That love and only love can
   Join the tribes of man.
   I would give my heart's desires
   So that you might see.
   The first step is to realize
   That it all begins with you and me. *(To Chorus)*

Call The Preacher

Words and Music by
Paul Overstreet

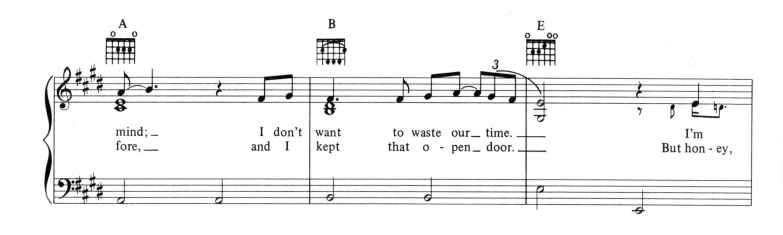

mind; __ I don't want to waste our __ time. __ I'm
fore, __ and I kept that o - pen __ door. __ But hon - ey,

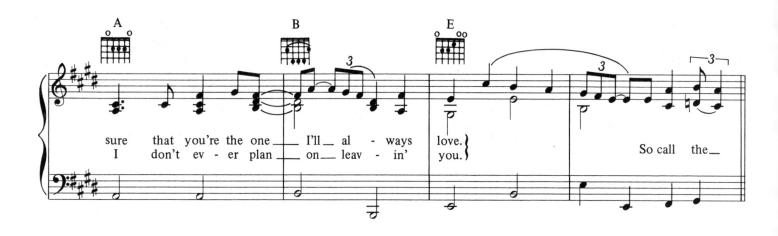

sure that you're the one __ I'll __ al - ways love.
I don't ev - er plan __ on __ leav - in' you. } So call the __

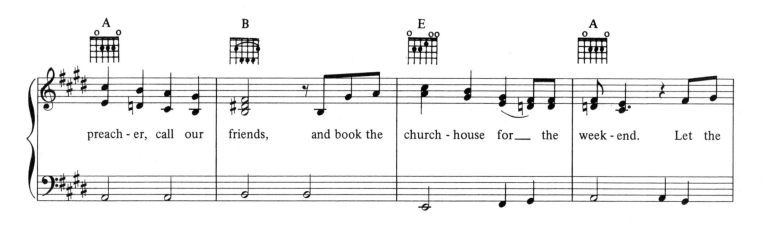

preach - er, call our friends, and book the church - house for __ the week - end. Let the

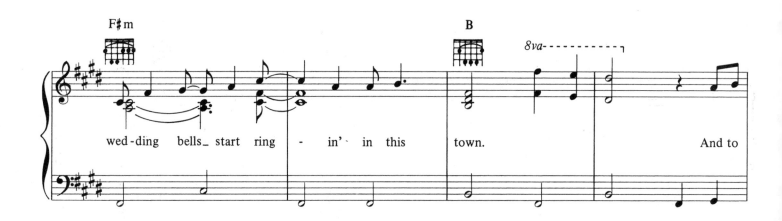

wed - ding bells __ start ring - in' in this town. And to

I Fell In Love With You For Life

Words and Music by
Dennis Morgan and Steve Davis

182

Additional Lyrics

2. The rose is for a season, summer always turns to fall,
So the way we live each moment is what matters most of all.
I live each day for your love, I swear it's forever true;
Every moment I'm given, I'll give back to you. *(To Chorus)*

The Keeper Of Your Heart

Words and Music by
Dennis Morgan and Steve Davis

If your love___ was a fad - ed rose,___ I'd be the sun-shine to make you grow.___ If you thirst - ed for rain,___ I'd be a riv - er that flows___ in - to your soul,___ and your col - ors would show.___ I'll be there to hold you in the night - time, build a for - tress

Chorus

Additional Lyrics

2. If your love was a rainy day,
   I'd be the wind and blow the clouds away,
   Be like the eye of a hurricane,
   And I'd shelter you from harm
   And keep you safe from the storm.
   So as time turns the pages of life,
   You can turn to me for the love that you need.
   With trust built on faith, we'll find security
   And the strength that we need
   To be the best that we can be. *(To Chorus)*

For You

Words and Music by
John Denver

Moderately

Just to look in your eyes a - gain, just to lay in your arms, just to be the first one al - ways there for you. Just to live in your laugh - ter,

just to sing   in your heart,

just to be ev -'ry one____

_____ of your dreams   come true.

Just to sit by your

win - dow,_____

morn - ing,_____

(mp)

just to touch   in the night,

just to you   by my side,

just to of - fer   a prayer   each   day   for you.

just to know that   you're nev - er   real - ly far   a - way.

Just to long for your kiss - es,_____ just to dream of your
Just a rea - son for liv - ing,_____ just to say I a -

sighs, just to know that I'd give my life for
dore, just to know that you're here in my heart to

you. } For you, all the rest__
stay. } *cresc.* *mf*

_ of my life._ For you, all the best_ of my life._ For

you a - lone,_____ on - ly for you. Just to wake up each
dim.

you.

Just the words of a love song, _____

just the beat of my heart, just the pledge of my life, _____

my love, for you.

rit. *a tempo* *rit.*

Perhaps Love

Words and Music by
John Denver

Angel Eyes

Words and Music by
John Hiatt and Fred Koller

Slow Rock Ballad

mf

1. Girl,_ you're look-ing_____ fine_____ to-night,_____ and ev-'ry guy has_ got you_

2.3. *See additional lyrics*

_ in _ his_ sight._____ What you're do-in' with a clown_____ like me_

is sure-ly one___ of life's___ lit-tle mys-ter-ies._____ So to-

Additional Lyrics

2. Well, I'm the guy who never learned to dance.
   Never even got one second glance.
   Across the crowded room was close enough.
   I could look but I could never touch. *(To Chorus)*

3. There's just one more thing I need to know:
   If this is love, why does it scare me so?
   It must be something only you can see,
   'Cause, girl, I feel it when you look at me. *(To Chorus)*

Recessional Music

Hallelujah Chorus

from *The Messiah*

George Frideric Handel

Allegro

Allegro

William Boyce

205

Voluntary On The Doxology (Old 100th)

Henry Purcell

Hornpipe

George Frideric Handel

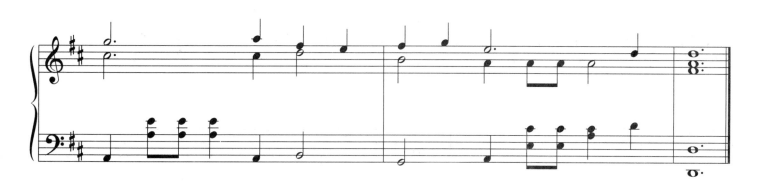

Fanfares

Jean-Joseph Mouret

Allegro vivace

Postlude Music

Adagio

from *Water Music Suite*

George Frideric Handel

Andante

from *Water Music Suite*

George Frideric Handel

Larghetto

George Frideric Handel

Prelude In C

from *The Well-Tempered Clavier, Part I*

Johann Sebastian Bach

Alphabetical
Contents

TRADITIONAL MUSIC

Adagio (from *Water Music Suite*)	Handel	218
Adagio (trans. by Bach)	Marcello	72
Air (from *Water Music Suite*)	Handel	10
Air	Mozart	31
Air On A G String	Bach	34
Allegro Maestoso	Handel	43
Allegro	Boyce	202
Amazing Grace	Traditional	20
Andante (from *Water Music Suite*)	Handel	220
Aria (Willst Du Dein Herz Mir Schenken)	Bach	70
Ave Maria (adapted by Gounod)	Bach	60
Ave Maria	Schubert	64
Be Thou With Me (Bist Du Bei Mir)	Bach	81
Bridal Chorus (from *Lohengrin*)	Wagner	38
Canon In D	Pachelbel	12
Chorale (from *Anna Magdalena Notebook*)	Bach	36
Elegie	Massenet	18
Fanfares	Mouret	214
Hallelujah Chorus (from *Messiah*)	Handel	200
Hornpipe	Handel	211
Jesu, Joy Of Man's Desiring	Bach	15
Larghetto	Handel	222
Lord's Prayer, The	Talbot	75
March	Handel	44
Minuet (from *Anna Magdalena Notebook*)	Bach	32
Minuets I & II	Purcell	26
My Faithful Heart (Mein Glaubiges Herz)	Bach	84
O Lord Most Holy (Panis Angelicus)	Franck	76

Prelude In C (from *The Well-Tempered Clavier, Part I*) Bach 224

Prince Of Denmark's March Clarke 46

Processional (from *Royal Fireworks Music*) Handel 47

Processional (from *Water Music Suite*) Handel 54

Processional (from *St. Anthony Chorale*) Haydn 48

Rondeau/The Masterpiece (arr. Parnes) Mouret 50

Sarabande (from *Anna Magdalena Notebook*) Bach 58

Sarabande In D Minor Handel 80

Sarabande In E Minor Handel 56

Sleepers, Wake Bach 22

Theme From Romeo And Juliet Tschaikovsky 28

Trumpet Tune Clarke 42

Voluntary On The Doxology (Old 100th) Purcell 206

Wedding March (from *A Midsummer Night's Dream*) Mendelssohn 40

CONTEMPORARY MUSIC

All My Life	Bonoff	163
Angel Eyes	Hiatt, Koller	196
Annie's Song	Denver	108
Battle Hymn Of Love, The	Overstreet, Schlitz	89
Call The Preacher	Overstreet	179
Everything True Love Touches	Alger, Sanders	128
For Sure, For Certain, Forever, For Always	Webb	106
For You	Denver	189
Forever And Ever, Amen	Overstreet, Schlitz	102
From This Moment On	Wildhorn, Goodrum	132
Goin' Gone	Koller, Alger, Dale	120
Hold On To The Nights	Marx	140
I Do	Alger, Longacre	124
I Do	Wildhorn	136
I Fell In Love With You For Life	Morgan, Davis	182
Keeper Of Your Heart, The	Morgan, Davis	185
Lady	Richie	112
Love Can Build A Bridge	Overstreet, Judd, Jarvis	174
Love Chooses You	Lewis	169
Love Of Loving You, The	Paxton	157
Love Until The End Of Time, A	Connors, Holdridge	93
May You Always	Markes, Charles	96
Melody Of Love	Glazer, Engelmann	100
My Treasure	Brown	116
Nobody Loves Me Like You Do	Phillips, Dunne	149
Perhaps Love	Denver	193
This Very Day	Overstreet, Elliott	166
Truly	Richie	160
We've Only Just Begun	Williams, Nichols	146
You Are So Beautiful	Preston, Fisher	154